WEIRD WILDLIFE

INSECTS

Anna Claybourne

Belitha Press

LOOK FOR THE BUG BOX

Look out for boxes like this with a little black bug in the corner. They contain extra info and amazing insect facts and figures.

Produced by
Monkey Puzzle Media Ltd,
Gissing's Farm, Fressingfield,
Suffolk IP21 5SH, UK

First published in the UK in 2002 by
Belitha Press Limited
An imprint of Chrysalis Books plc,
64 Brewery Road,
London N7 9NT, UK

Copyright © Belitha Press Ltd 2001

Designer: Tim Mayer
Editor: Jason Hook
Consultant: Joyce Pope

ISBN 1 84138 359 7

British Library Cataloguing in Publication Data for this book is available from the British Library.

Printed in Hong Kong
10 9 8 7 6 5 4 3 2 1

Acknowledgements
We wish to thank the following individuals and organizations for their help and assistance and for supplying material in their collections: Bruce Coleman Collection front cover (MPL Fogden), back cover bottom left (Stephen J Krasemann), 4 bottom (MPL Fogden), 8 top (Stephen J Krasemann), 9 (Gerald S Cubitt), 29 (Kim Taylor); Corbis 16-17 (Kevin Schafer), 27 (Layne Kennedy); FLPA 18 top (Minden Pictures); MPM Images back cover top, 18-19; NHPA back cover bottom right (Michael Tweedie), 3 (GJ Cambridge), 5 (ANT), 6 top (James Carmichael Jr), 6 bottom (Anthony Bannister), 12 (Daniel Heuclin), 13 top (Anthony Bannister), 13 bottom (GJ Cambridge), 14 top (Stephen Dalton), 14 bottom (Robert Thompson), 17 bottom (Anthony Bannister), 19 top (Anthony Bannister), 20 (Anthony Bannister), 23 bottom (Stephen Dalton), 24 top (Michael Tweedie), 26 (Stephen Dalton), 31 (Stephen Dalton); Oxford Scientific Films 1 (Konrad Wothe), 2 (David M Dennis), 4 top (Wendy Shattil/Bob Rozinski), 7 (John Weeber/Hedgehog House), 8 bottom (GI Bernard), 10 (HL Fox), 11 top (Konrad Wothe), 11 bottom (P&W Ward), 15 (Satoshi Kuribayashi), 21 top (David Thompson), 21 bottom (Satoshi Kuribayashi), 22 (David Dennis/ Animals Animals), 23 top (JAL Cooke), 24 bottom (GI Bernard), 25 (David M Dennis), 30 (JAL Cooke), 28 (Densey Cline/Mantis Wildlife Films).

▼ These hungry cockroaches are tucking into a half-eaten sandwich.

► A close-up photograph of the feathery antennae (feelers) of an emperor moth.

CONTENTS

THE WEIRD WORLD OF INSECTS

Insects are everywhere! They live below ground, inside houses, underwater, on plants and even on other animals. For every human being alive on Earth, there are over a billion insects.

◄ There are millions of aphids like these in an average field.

▼ This lantern bug lives in the steamy forests of Malaysia.

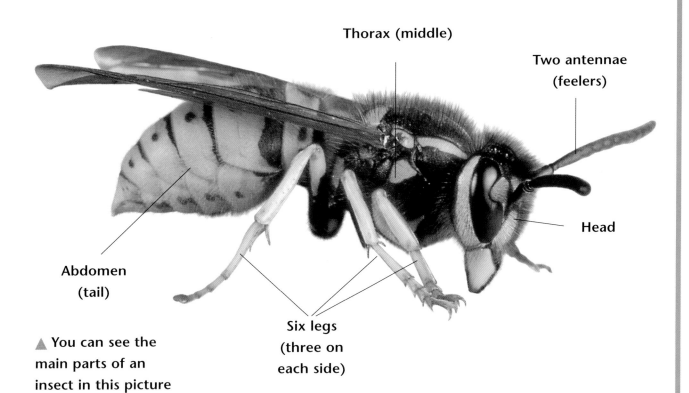

Thorax (middle)

Two antennae (feelers)

Head

Abdomen (tail)

Six legs (three on each side)

▲ You can see the main parts of an insect in this picture of a wasp. Not all insects have wings.

IS IT AN INSECT?

Not all creepy-crawlies are insects. All insects have six legs and two feelers. Creatures with eight legs, such as spiders, are not really insects. Nor are slugs and worms, because they have no legs at all!

Why are there so many insects? The answer is that they have found so many weird ways of living. They eat many different kinds of food, from wooden furniture to plant pollen to elephant dung. Some insects can disguise themselves to hide from enemies. Others use powerful weapons and clever tricks to stay alive.

How can you spot an insect? All insects, when they are fully grown, have six legs. Their bodies are divided into three parts. They also have two feelers on their heads, called antennae.

Insects do not have bones inside their bodies like us. Instead, they have a hard, tough outer skin. This protects their soft insides. As they get larger, they lose this skin and grow a new one.

STRANGE SHAPES

Some insects look very strange. Sometimes being a weird shape can help an insect to find food. Other insects look ugly or frightening so that they can scare their enemies away.

If you had eyes on stalks like the diopsid fly at the bottom of the page, you could use them to peek round corners! But diopsid flies do not do this. Instead, they fight each other by holding up their eye-stalks. The fly with the longest stalks is the winner.

▼ Peanut-head bugs live in rainforests and eat tree sap. Their large heads may help to frighten other animals away.

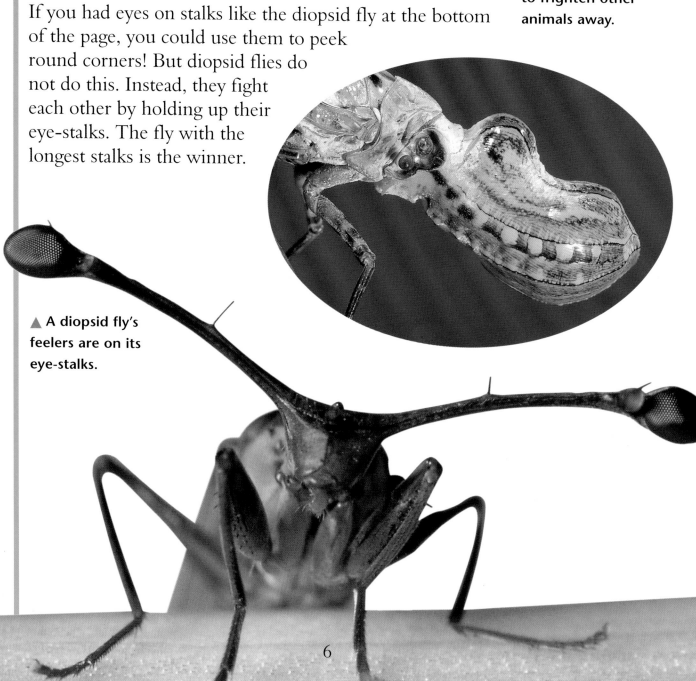

▲ A diopsid fly's feelers are on its eye-stalks.

You can tell a lot about weird insects from their names. The peanut-head bug gets its name from its strangely shaped head, which looks like a peanut shell. Giraffe weevils, from Africa, are little beetles with very long necks. No one knows why they have them.

Some insects have strange body parts to help them reach their food. Butterflies and moths have a long, thin tube in their mouth called a proboscis. They use it like a drinking straw to suck a sweet juice called nectar out of flowers. The Darwin's hawk-moth has a very long proboscis, so it can suck nectar from its favourite orchid.

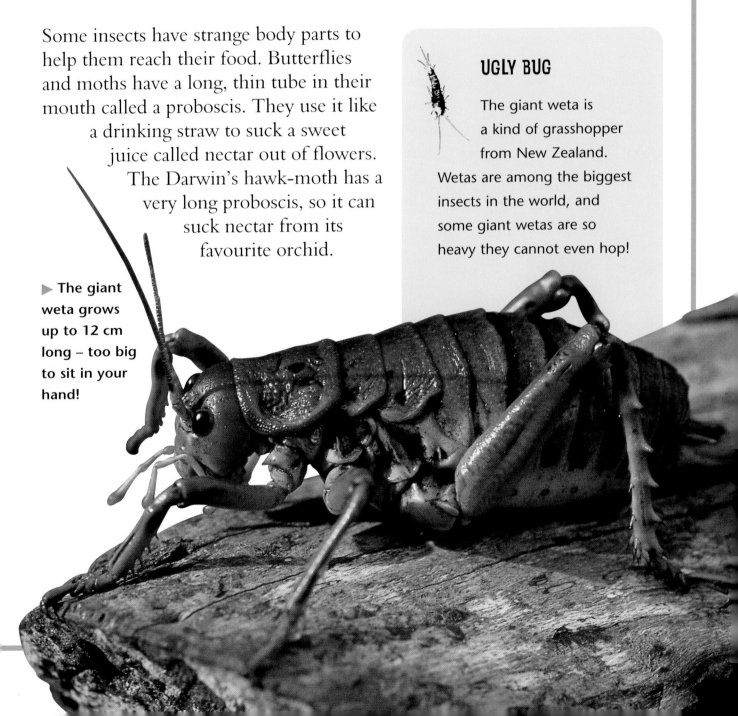

UGLY BUG

The giant weta is a kind of grasshopper from New Zealand. Wetas are among the biggest insects in the world, and some giant wetas are so heavy they cannot even hop!

▶ The giant weta grows up to 12 cm long – too big to sit in your hand!

DARING DISGUISES

Camouflage means disguising yourself so that it is harder for your enemies to see you. Insects are experts at camouflage. They can make themselves look like leaves, flowers, twigs, tree bark, other animals or even bird-droppings!

Insects can sometimes avoid being eaten, by looking like the plants they live on. Some insects are amazingly good at this. The Indian leaf butterfly and the Javanese leaf insect look exactly like leaves. It is very hard to see them, even if you look carefully. They had better watch out for animals that eat leaves!

▲ This scary 'snake' is in fact the tail end of a hawk-moth caterpillar.

Stick insects look like the green stems of plants, thorn bugs look like thorns, and some caterpillars look just like a bird-dropping. Not many animals would want to eat that!

▶ How many stick insects can you spot on this plant?

Some insects disguise themselves as something much bigger and scarier than themselves, like a small bird or lizard. This is another good way to stop an enemy gobbling you up. The owl butterfly has spots on its wings that look like the eyes of a large owl. Owls are deadly hunters. So, a hungry lizard that thinks it sees an owl's face staring at it will keep away.

► The abdomen of this leaf insect from Malaysia dangles down just like a real leaf.

MOTH BURGERS

Insects need camouflage because lots of animals love to eat them. Other insects, birds, fish, frogs, lizards and larger animals such as anteaters all enjoy eating insects. In many countries, people eat them too! Fried locusts, chocolate-covered ants and moth burgers are all eaten in different parts of the world.

DISGUSTING DINERS

Insects have two main types of mouth. Some have a long, thin proboscis for sucking up liquids. Others have jaws called mandibles, which they use for biting.

Many insects need to turn solid food into a liquid before they can eat it. The assassin bug attacks a smaller insect by stabbing it with a long, sharp proboscis. Then it injects special spit that turns the victim's insides to jelly. The assassin bug sucks up the jelly, leaving the empty insect skin behind.

▼ An assassin bug from Africa attacking an unlucky cockroach.

Some insects eat members of their own family. A baby gall-midge lives inside its mother, and eats her from the inside out!

Female praying mantises are bigger than males. When they have mated, the male needs to escape. Otherwise, the female bites the male's head off and eats him.

▲ This picture shows a close-up of the sucker-shaped mouth of a common housefly.

▼ This female praying mantis is halfway through eating her mate.

SUPER SENSES

▼ This emperor dragonfly has more than 30 000 separate eyes in each compound eye.

Some insects are much better than you at hearing, seeing, tasting and smelling. But they sometimes do these things in weird ways. Butterflies can taste with their feet, moths can sniff with their feelers and grasshoppers can hear with their knees!

Butterflies, bees and some flies and moths can taste with their feet. This is very useful, because it means they can tell straight away whether they have landed on something that is good to eat. Bees and butterflies also find their food by sight and smell.

Insect ears are even weirder. Some grasshoppers hear with pads shaped like drums on the sides of their knees. They use these to listen for other grasshoppers. Some moths have ears on the sides of their body, which they use to listen for bats that like to eat them.

SUPER SNIFFERS

● Ants find their way home by following trails of smelly scent left by other ants from their nest.

● A male Indian moon-moth can smell a female, using his feelers, from up to 11 kilometres away.

▶ This type of grasshopper has ears on its sides. The ear is the pale oval patch just below the wing.

If you take a close look at a fly or dragonfly, you will notice its big, bulging eyes. Eyes like these are made up of thousands of tiny eyes, all joined together. They are called compound eyes. These eyes are so powerful that they can see the slightest movements. They also allow insects such as dragonflies to look in all directions when they are hunting.

▼ Many moths have amazingly sensitive antennae for sniffing out a mate.

WEIRD WEAPONS

Like humans, many insects use weapons. But insects have their weapons built into their bodies. They use nasty sprays, painful stings or giant pincers to fight their enemies.

Many insects have strong jaws shaped like pincers. Sometimes these pincers are so large they can be used as weapons. Male stag-beetles use their giant jaws to have wrestling matches. Soldier ants also have huge jaws for fighting off animals that attack their nest.

▲ In this wrestling match, one stag-beetle has managed to lift the other off the ground.

STING IN THE TAIL

Bees, wasps and some flies defend themselves by stinging. But when a honeybee stings you, it dies soon afterwards. So why does it do it? Bees do not sting to defend themselves, but to protect the other bees in their group, or colony. A few bees will die to save the rest.

▲ Dragonfly larvae (babies) have huge biting jaws for grabbing and killing their prey.

Bombardier beetles have a spray that is not only poisonous, but boiling hot as well.
The bombardier has a hole inside its body, near its tail. When danger threatens, substances in the beetle's body are mixed together in this hole. They make a poisonous gas which the beetle can squirt in any direction.

▲ This bombardier beetle is squirting its gas after being poked.

If you come across an American walking stick, you had better leave it alone. It is a weird kind of insect. When disturbed, it sprays a painful liquid into its enemy's eyes. The spray can blind the enemy for several minutes, which is long enough for the walking stick to escape.

▲ Killer bees look like normal bees, but they are much nastier.

KILLER CREATURES

Insects may be tiny, but some of them can kill humans and large animals. Mosquitoes and tsetse flies kill by spreading deadly diseases. Killer bees gang up together, and sting their victims to death.

Killer bees are a type of honeybee from Africa. They spread to South America when scientists took them to Brazil to try to breed a new type of bee that would make lots of honey. But their experiment went wrong, and they ended up with bad-tempered bees instead!

Killer bees form a big swarm to chase their victims and sting them many times. Their stings are no worse than other bee stings. But if you are stung too many times, you can die.

THE LAST BITES

Hundreds of years ago, millions of people died from a terrible disease called the Black Death. It was spread by bites from fleas!

The deadliest insects of all are mosquitoes. They spread a disease called malaria, which kills millions of people every year. Mosquitoes bite people and animals to suck their blood. When they do this, they inject spit which contains germs.

▲ This tsetse fly is feeding on human blood. It could be giving someone sleeping sickness.

COOL COLONIES

▼ These leafcutter ants are taking pieces of leaf back to their nest to use as food.

Some insects live in big groups called colonies. There can be millions of ants, bees, wasps or termites in one colony. They all help each other live together.

In a hive of honeybees, there are three types of bee. Each one has a different job. The queen lays eggs to make new bees for the hive. Male bees called drones mate with the queen. Then there are female bees called workers, who have lots of jobs. They collect nectar, make honey and care for babies. They even fan the hive with their wings to keep it cool.

SMELLY TALK

How do colony insects know what to do and where to go? Some experts think that the insects can 'talk' to each other by using special smells that have different meanings. When a bee uses its sting, it makes a smell that warns other bees of danger.

18

Colony insects usually build themselves a home to share. Ants dig tunnels, bees build a nest from wax, and wasps make a home from chewed-up wood.

Some termites build amazing towers out of soil and termite spit. Inside the towers, the termites dig a complicated system of tunnels and rooms. A termite tower can be taller than a giraffe and contain more than five million termites. They are all brothers and sisters!

▼ The termite queen weighs as much as 100 worker termites, and is so fat she cannot move.

▼ This wide, lumpy termite mound has a tower sticking out of the top.

MARVELLOUS MESSAGES

Insects cannot talk like we do, but they can send each other messages in all kinds of ways. Some of these are so clever that scientists do not really understand how they work.

ROBOT BEE

Scientists in Germany made a robot bee and used it to send signals to real bees. By making the robot bee dance and buzz its wings, they could send the other bees in any direction they liked.

In a hot country, you might hear a noise that sounds like an electric saw. It is a cicada, the world's noisiest insect. Male cicadas make this noise with pads on the sides of their body, which are like the skin on a drum. The male cicada vibrates these very quickly, making a noise to call females.

Insects called fireflies signal to their mates by glowing. Males fly around at night, flashing a light on their bodies. Females on the ground flash their light to answer. Different types of firefly flash their lights in different patterns.

▼ Cicadas are big, fat and very noisy!

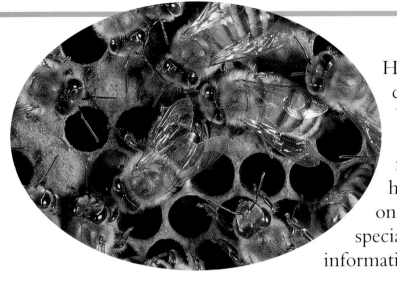

Honeybees can send very detailed messages to each other. When a worker bee finds a good patch of flowers, she needs to tell the other bees in her hive about it. So she lands on the honeycomb and does a special dance that contains all the information they need.

▲ As one honeybee does her dance around the hive, the others follow her closely to find out what she's telling them.

▼ When lots of fireflies flash their lights together, they can look like a beautiful firework display.

WEIRD WATER INSECTS

Some insects live in ponds, streams, rivers or the sea. They have lots of weird ways of staying safe, catching food and breathing underwater.

Many water insects do not live in the water, they live on it! Pond-skaters and water-striders walk on the surface of ponds, hunting other small creatures. They can do this because water has a kind of 'skin' on the surface. This skin is made by tiny droplets of water, called molecules, clinging together. It is strong enough to hold up small animals or objects.

▼ You can see this pond-skater's feet are making dents in the skin on the water's surface.

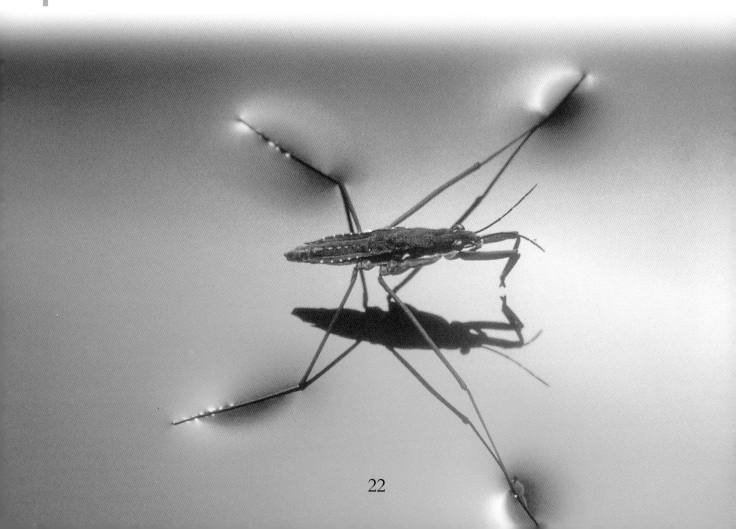

These mosquito babies, called larvae, are underwater. They are breathing through tubes that reach the water's surface.

Sea-skaters live on the surface of the ocean in the same way. They have to find floating objects such as feathers, so that they can lay their eggs on them.

Some baby water insects have gills for breathing underwater, just like a fish. Other insects have to come to the surface to breathe. Diving-beetles catch a bubble of air and carry it underwater with them. Water-scorpions and baby mosquitoes have breathing tubes, like straws, which reach up to the surface.

▶ You can see the ripples left by the whirligig beetles as they twirl around on the water.

DOUBLE VISION

Whirligig beetles swim around on the surface of the water in spiral patterns. Their eyes are split into two parts. One part looks above the surface, and the other looks underwater!

◀ Silverfish are insects, but they look a bit like tiny, shiny fish. They live in damp corners of houses.

HORRIBLE HOUSEMATES

▼ A death-watch beetle sits among the remains of household wood that it has chewed.

Who shares your house with you? Apart from your family, there could be thousands of weird insects crawling around under the floorboards, in your furniture and in your food cupboards!

Instead of eating outdoor plants and creatures, some insects have learned to live on things found in your home.

Carpet-beetles eat woollen carpets, clothes moths nibble on jumpers, and book lice eat the glue that holds old books together.

▼ Cockroaches feasting on a left-over sandwich.

HEADLESS HORRORS

Cockroaches are incredibly tough. They can survive even if they are wet or freezing cold. They can also live for up to a month without their heads!

The spookiest household insects are death-watch beetles, which tunnel through wooden beams and furniture. They knock their jaws against the sides of their tunnels to make a tapping noise. Long ago, people believed this noise meant someone in the house was about to die.

The insects most people hate to see in their house are cockroaches. These large insects hide in dark corners and come out to eat people's left-overs. They look scary and can run faster than any other insect. They also make a horrible smell. Cockroaches are hard to get rid of because they are amazingly tough. They can live for months without eating.

WEIRD-INSECT FACTS

Big bugs

The longest insect in the world is the giant stick insect from Indonesia. It can be 50 cm long, including its feelers. The heaviest insect is the Goliath beetle from Africa, which weighs up to 100g.

Wide wings

The great owlet moth, the Australian Hercules moth and the Queen Alexandra's birdwing butterfly are the insects with the biggest wings. They have wingspans of about 30 cm, the size of a dinner plate.

▼ A cat flea takes off on its death-defying jump.

Wee wasp

The smallest insect is a type of tiny wasp that lives on other insects' eggs. It is only about 0.2 mm long.

Motor moth

The fastest insect flight ever measured was made by a hawk-moth which reached a speed of 53.6 km/h.

Running roach

Cockroaches can run at 30 cm per second. This might not seem very fast, but it's not bad when you think that the cockroach is only 3 cm long. If you could run at the same speed for your size, you would be running at 32 km/h.

Flea flips

Fleas are the highest jumpers. They can jump 200 times the length of their own bodies. If you could do the same, you could jump over a block of flats.

Busy butterfly

Butterflies called painted ladies travel very long distances every year. Some make journeys of over 6400 km, from northern Africa to northern Europe.

Whirring wings

A midge is a little insect with a nasty bite. One type of midge can beat its wings faster than any other insect – over 1000 times every second.

Tottering termite

Termites can live longer than any other insect. The queen of a termite colony can sometimes live for up to 50 years. But worker and soldier termites live to be only four or five years old.

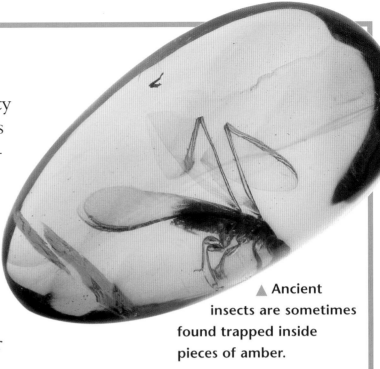

▲ Ancient insects are sometimes found trapped inside pieces of amber.

Chirpy cicada

The loudest insect is the cicada. The male's drumming noises can be heard up to 2 km away.

Murdering mosquito

The deadliest insect has to be the mosquito. Malaria, the disease mosquitoes spread, has killed millions of people throughout history. Scientists think that half of all the people who have ever died, have died from malaria.

Insect invasion

It is hard to say how many insects there are altogether, because there are too many to count. Experts believe there are about 10 quintillion (10 000 000 000 000 000 000) insects alive at any one time.

Spreading species

Scientists have discovered about a million different sorts, or species, of insect. They think there may be 10 million more species that we do not even know about yet. Around five new sorts are found every day.

Ant army

There are probably more ants on the Earth than any other insect. Some experts think that if you weighed all the ants on Earth, they would weigh more than all the humans put together.

Backward bugs

A few insect species, including hover-flies and dragonflies, can fly backwards. They can also hover in mid-air like a helicopter.

WEIRD-INSECT WORDS

This glossary explains some of the unusual words in this book.

Abdomen
The tail part of an insect's body. It is usually the largest of an insect's three body parts.

Antennae
The two stalks on an insect's head which it uses for feeling and smelling. They are also called feelers.

Camouflage
Colours, shapes or patterns which help an insect to disguise itself and hide from enemies.

Colony
A group of insects, such as bees, ants or wasps, that live together and help each other to survive.

Compound eye
A kind of large insect eye made up of many smaller eyes joined together. It is easy to see compound eyes in butterflies or grasshoppers.

Drone
A male honeybee.

Gills
Parts of the body which allow some insects to breathe underwater. Sometimes gills are feathery parts on the tail.

Honeycomb
The waxy structure inside a bee's nest. Honeycomb is made up of thousands of chambers called cells. They are shaped like hexagons.

Larva
A kind of baby insect that looks a bit like a short, fat worm. Bees, flies and beetles all produce a baby called a larva.

Mandibles
Biting, clamping jaws, which some insects such as ants and praying mantises have.

▲ These honeypot ants are using their bodies as storage jars to hold food for the rest of their colony.

ALL FOR ONE AND ONE FOR ALL

Ants, honeybees, wasps and termites all live for their colony. A single insect is happy to die to save all the others in their colony. Some scientists say that insects in a colony do not really act on their own. A colony of insects is really like a single animal, with many separate parts.

▲ **These worker wasps are looking after their eggs and babies.**

Mates
A pair of insects who make babies together are known as mates. The way they make babies is called mating.

Molecules
Molecules are the tiny parts that make up any substance. Water in a river, wood in a table or the paper in this book are all made up of molecules.

Nectar
A sweet juice found inside flowers. Many insects, such as bees and butterflies, feed on nectar.

Pincers
A pair of claws or jaws that work by pressing against each other.

Pollen
A yellow powder made by flowers. Flowers swap pollen with each other to make seeds.

Proboscis
A part of the mouth used for sucking up liquids. Insects such as mosquitoes and bugs have a proboscis.

Queen
A large, female insect. The queen is the most important member of a colony of insects, such as bees, ants or termites. The queen lays eggs to make new insects for the colony.

Sap
A sticky juice made by trees.

Species
A group or type of insect, given a special name by scientists.

Spiral
Shaped or moving in the form of a coil or spring.

Thorax
The middle of the three parts of an insect's body, between the head and the abdomen. An insect's legs, and its wings if it has any, grow from its thorax.

Vibration
Movement back and forth very fast, often to make a sound. Cicadas make a noise by vibrating patches of skin on their sides.

Worker
Most of the ants, bees, wasps or termites in an insect colony are workers. They do all the tasks such as collecting food, protecting the nest and caring for babies. Worker insects are usually female.

WEIRD-INSECT PROJECTS

Here are some ideas for discovering more about weird insects. Try these insect projects and activities.

BUTTERFLY WORLD

Many towns and cities have a Butterfly World centre. These are like small zoos where visitors can see beautiful butterflies from all over the world. The butterflies are usually kept in a large, glass house with lots of plants. You can walk around as they fly through the air. Sometimes they may even land on your head. Some centres also have ants, cockroaches and stick insects for you to look at. To find your nearest one, look for Butterfly World in your telephone directory.

INSECT SPOTTING

You can find insects in most outdoor places, especially in the summer. Here are some of the best places to look. Remember to be careful when you are insect spotting. Do not touch any insects, in case they bite or sting. And make sure you have an adult with you when you go near ponds or rivers.

Leaf litter

Piles of old, dead leaves are a great place to see insects. Look underneath damp leaves from the bottom of the pile. You might see beetles, or perhaps insect eggs waiting to hatch.

▶ This is a springtail, a type of tiny jumping insect often found in leaf litter, soil and compost.

Parks and gardens

In summer, watch flowering plants closely to see honeybees and butterflies collecting nectar and pollen. Beetles often crawl on trees or across pathways.

Ponds and rivers

Look carefully at the surface of ponds and pools to spot pond-skaters or whirligig beetles. Collect a jar full of pond water and look through the glass to see if there are any water insects inside. Make sure you pour them back afterwards.

WEIRD INSECTS ON THE WEB

If you have a computer, you can search the Internet for websites about weird insects from all over the world. Remember that websites change, so do not worry if you cannot find all these sites. You can find other sites by using the name of your favourite insect as a searchword. You might try 'ant' or 'butterfly'.

The Wonderful World of Insects

www.insectworld.com/insects/six.html
Facts, book reviews and information about clubs and societies.

University of Kentucky Entomology Department

www.uky.edu/Agriculture/Entomology
/ythfacts/bugfood/bugfood.htm
All about insects as food for humans.

KEEPING STICK INSECTS

The sites below have tips on keeping stick insects as pets.

Cyber Sticks!

www.cybersticks.co.uk/
keepingstickinsects.htm
Everything you need to know about keeping stick insects.

The Care of Stick Insects

www.earthlife.net/insects/
sticks.html
How and where to keep stick insects.

▶ A white-tailed bumblebee visits a foxglove flower to collect nectar and pollen.

INDEX